HOW TO
DRESS
FOR EVERY OCCASION
BY THE POPE

WITH ORIGINAL ILLUSTRATIONS
BY SARAH "PINKIE" BENNETT

McSWEENEY'S IRREGULARS
SAN FRANCISCO

For more information about McSweeney's, visit www.mcsweeneys.net.

ISBN: 1-932416-41-2

HOW TO
DRESS
FOR EVERY OCCASION
BY THE POPE

WITH ORIGINAL ILLUSTRATIONS
BY SARAH "PINKIE" BENNETT

To You Know Who.
—T. P.

To the Pope, for believing.
—S. "P." B.

INTRODUCTION

HELLO, I'M THE POPE.

How many times have you opened your closet and got real nervous? A lot, I bet!! Dressing well (or "looking your best") is one of the biggest concerns of people today, and for a good reason ... If you don't look your best, people won't think the best of you, and this can lead to all sorts of trouble. Careless or messy outfits will win you disrespect. Not paying attention to what you're wearing can cause trouble with your peers and friends. And sometimes you'll find that you're wearing an outfit that's just plain wrong. History and society has proved this dozens of times.

But not me!! I've lost track of the number of times people have said to me, "Your Holiness, you look like a million bucks." I always mind my manners and say "thank you!"—but deep in my heart I think it's easy. Well, hang onto your hats!! Because Today is the day that I share my secrets of snappy (and appropriate!!) dressing to you. This is a book you can take with you to the closet or dresser drawer, because I'm going to tell you *exactly* what to wear no matter what. Whether you're a busy man or wife in the city, or the Pope, you'll be "ready for the world" thanks to these pretty-easy-to-remember tips. The book is divided into chapters so you can look things up ... and look your best!!

Are you ready?? Well let's go!!!! Dressing well is an adventure and clothing is the star!!

✚ **pope tip** *Don't rush through the book!!! There are secrets of super dressing on every page.*

1

THE BASICS

OK, NOW YOU'RE SAYING, "I'm ready, the Pope! Tell me everything!!!" Well, hold on!! You can't just wake up one morning and be a better dresser for every occasion. A journey begins with a million steps, and the first step is the step I like to call "The Basics." In this chapter we'll learn all the Basics of dressing so we can know what we're talking about!!! (In the other chapters.)

NUMBER ONE: THE HAT

FIRST OFF, GET A BIG HAT as shown. If you're going to dress well from head to toe, WHY NOT START WITH THE HEAD??? A big hat on your head says to everybody, "Guess who's in charge?" I'll give you a hint:

The Hat: *You can get this from a catalogue!*

It's you if you're wearing an impressive hat. Hats come in all sorts of shapes but this shape is the best. Hats keep you hot in winter and shady during the summer due to the unique fabric. I get my hats personally from a catalog but don't be shy—shop around!!!

NUMBER TWO: A ROBE

OK, LET'S NOT MAKE JOKES—you know we're not talking about the bathrobes you already own!! Bathrobes make you look sloppy—like you don't care enough to put on anything special, just an ordinary bathrobe. The shinier the fabric the more of an impression you will make each and every time you wear the robe. The adjective in your head when you look at the robe should be: "regal." Regal or Royal is not just who you are if you're in a very important position—it's the outfit you have on. And the robe is *very key*.

Note also the stitching. There should be fancy patterns and particularly beadwork. Let's face it—hand-stitching is the best!! But of course many people can't afford it and they can't find it either. Quite frankly,

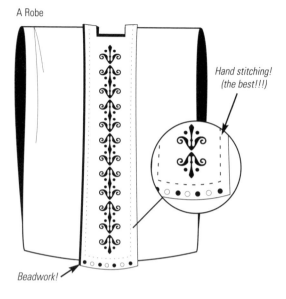

A Robe

Hand stitching! (the best!!!)

Beadwork!

the answer is: Save up. Because a cheap robe is just going to look like a cheap robe, and it will change the "mental adjective" to: cheapie.

OK, on to the next thing.

A NICE TUNIC

NOW, THIS IS SOMETHING that's a little more understated than the other Basics so far. The reason is: it goes underneath the robe and really only "peeks out," so if price is a concern (and who isn't these days!!) it's A-OK to have a slightly cheaper tunic with just simple stitching. Of course, the tunic isn't invisible—lots of people are going to see it, sooner or later, no matter what! So personally I like the ones with some stitching on them. It can be a design or whatever—nothing tacky like "Go Knicks!" or even a monogram because that just confuses people and distracts them from

4

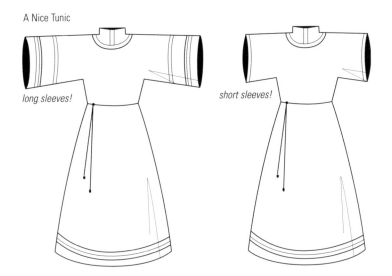

A Nice Tunic

long sleeves! *short sleeves!*

the issue. Short sleeves or long sleeves is your choice but personally (ATTENTION!!! PERSONAL OPINION COMING UP!!!) I like long sleeves in the winter and short in the summer because of the weather.

Got it? OK, let's move on to ...

NUMBER FOUR: A SCEPTER STAFF OR STICK

I CAN ALMOST HEAR what you're saying in my head: "Your Worship, is one of those big jewelled sticks really part of the outfit? It's more like a prop, am I right?" Are you right? NO! I don't mean to be bossy, but think about it: if you're *always carrying a stick,* people are going to automatically "assume" that it's part of the impression you are trying to give. Yes, it can be a pain to carry around sometimes. Yes, it comes in different sizes. Yes, it probably should be jewelled, and you'd be surprised at the number of people who know whether it's a real jewel or some fake thing you got at one of those stores. (Again: the word "cheapie.")

Now, I know I'm going to get a lot of crap for this, but I gotta say, for antiques like scepter sticks, Italy is the best. There's something about an ancient civilization that can produce such VERY BEAUTIFUL items. If you want a scepter staff, or any kind of big stick, whether it has a curve on top (I like that!!) or just regular (that's OK too!!) the word quality is spelled I-T-A-L-Y. Have your attendants look in all of the best Italian stores and museums. Choose carefully but not too carefully—you don't want to waste your life shopping for the scepter staff. And don't forget to say "thank you."

NUMBER FIVE: FANCY SHOES

THEY DON'T HAVE TO curl up at the toe like in the picture. (By the way, Thanks Pinkie!!!!!) But they should be fancy so probably there's going to be something on the toe, whether it's a miniature (emphasize the word "MINIATURE"!!) pom-pom or a bell or little tassels. The main thing is, it's a shoe that looks delicate and fancy at the same time. Sayonara, hiking boots!!! Many people say, "Who's going to notice shoes, Your Grace?" but my answer is always the same: "absolutely everybody in the whole church or wherever." Someone's walking in a procession, eventually you're going to look down at the shoes, especially if you're sitting in the aisle. It's natural.

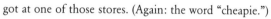

A Scepter Stick: *Consider one from ITALY!!!!!*

Fancy Shoes

Try a pom-pom, a bell or a little tassel!!!

Some people say that a soft, fancy shoe is really more of a slipper, but slipper, shoe, whatever you want to say, GET SOME!

BOWL OF INCENSE

If you want.
(Optional.)

Bowl of Incense *(if you want)*

RINGS!!

I CAN'T BELIEVE I almost forgot to say rings. You want a bunch of them, all precious, on the main fingers of both your hands. Some of the rings have special significance which we'll get to if we have time, but the point is: rings. After all, when people kneel down to kiss your rings, if you're not wearing rings ... I can't even think about it, quite frankly! Talk about falling on your face!!!

IN CONCLUSION, those are "the basics" for right way dressing. Now get ready

Rings!!!

to see these clothings in action as we move on to ... the other chapters!

✣ **pope tip** *Take a list with you when you shop.*

AT WORK

THERE IS NO OTHER place to be taken more seriously as a professional than at work. Office, Vatican, whatever, people are going to be watching you and judging you as a professional who does their job. Overalls is not what we're talking about here. Blue jeans are not welcome, and don't give me some big speech about how fancy they are!! If you're at work, you want the whole shebang: hat, robe, tunic, fancy slippers. And don't forget the scepter staff!! Hold it *under your arm* when you're getting coffee and you shouldn't have a problem.

"Hello Guiseppe!" "Hello Your Holiness! Wow, even on a regular workday you are wearing so many rings!!" "I know!" This is the sort of conversation that proves my tips are working. And a firm handshake makes that extra-clear.

If you haven't already, get an antique wooden stand to hold your hat when you're sitting at your big desk. If the hat falls off when you're holding a fancy pen and the ink squirts every old place, that's Goodbye Edict!

Watch that pen!

TO CHURCH

OUT OF ALL THE PLACES in the world, church can be the fanciest. Don't worry, I understand—it's tough to maintain a balance between looking very fancy but not looking like you're thinking it's all about you. After all, the Church is holy—and we can't ever forget that!! That's why you want to wear a robe with *very fancy stitching*, a big hat, a scepter stick, fancy shoes or slippers and a tunic underneath ... and let's face it: this is the time to open up your ring box and put rings all over your fingers. It's Church if you know what I mean!!! Archbishops and everybody will have incense so that's one thing you don't have to worry about. If you dress like I'm telling you it almost doesn't matter what you say, but nevertheless you want to prepare your blessings. Some of the other priests can help—it's their job!!

✚ **pope tip** *Everybody is going to be looking at you. It's part of your job to look your very best in church. Show you care— dress snappy.*

AT PLAY

WORKTIME IS NO TIME for play and vice versa. Just like you don't use Latin at the gelato stand you don't lead a procession when you're sitting around the yard. But, the trouble is, you never know. So just in case you want to have all the Basics covered: a robe, a hat, with the tunic underneath (short sleeves in hot weather and vice versa) and some fancy shoes on your feet. See how the little curled up toes work even in a "play" situation? That's what I mean by versatile.

"The Pope, the Pope, aren't you forgetting rings and a scepter stick???" No, I am not. Put those both on, no matter what anybody else says.

If it's very hot out—and in Italy that's during the summer and other warmer months—you can have someone stand behind you with a sort of fancy umbrella type thing to keep you in the shade at all times. It's totally worth it!!

✣ **pope tip** *I don't care who says so, NO SANDALS!! This isn't a beach party we're talking about.*

Listen in the privacy of your own chambers!
I like music from ITALY.

THE NIGHTLIFE

HERE WE MIGHT HAVE some sort of conflict problems. My personal opinion is that you're not going to get ahead in this world if you get into the nightlife. (One bishop sees you and it's kaput!!) Plus places like nightclubs and discos are "not my style" and I don't think they're your style either, frankly. So you're never going to see this Holiness out there, endangering people with his big stick or scepter or whatever!! Dancing with that thing?? No way José!!!

But if you insist, I'm just going to say that you still want the robe, a tunic underneath, the big hat and some fancy shoes for that fancy footwork you insist on doing at all hours. If smoking isn't allowed probably incense isn't either although I don't think Italy has the anti-smoking thing as much. Remember, though ... fancy robes means fancy cloth, and fancy cloth means STAINS!! Don't come crying to me if somebody jostles you and there's a big splash of wine down the middle. "Your Holiness, Your Holiness!!!" "I warned you!!! I warned you but you wouldn't listen!!!" That's the dark side of the nightlife.

✣ **pope tip** *If you go to discos for the music, there's nothing wrong with buying a CD or two and listening the privacy of your own chambers! Italy has some wonderful record stores that often give a discount if you're a personage of some sort. Again, this is where dressing your best comes into play.*

WEDDINGS & PICNICS

BOTH OF THESE CAN be (but not always!) outdoors, so a lot of people say, "Your Holiness, can I wear sandals??" HELLO?!?!?!? Are you even reading this book? NO SANDALS and THAT IS FINAL. For a wedding, you want to look your best even if you aren't personally blessing the wedding couple: I'm talking about the robe with the tunic underneath, fancy shoes, a scepter stick and a big tall hat to show everybody that you are respectful of the occasion. This might be one time when the robe shouldn't be white because it's the bride's special day, but on the other hand wearing white will show that you recognize the holiness and specialty of the day, so it's a toss-up in terms of wearing white or not. Your choice!! Same thing with picnics except they tend to be more casual. Still, I'll say it again: with lots of rings you CANNOT LOSE!

✛ **pope tip** *Don't show off. If you want to buy from the registry, fine. Or you can go to some antique stores and get them a tasteful antiquity. Don't spend a bundle—that always comes back to haunt you! Italy has the best stores for this kind of thing.*

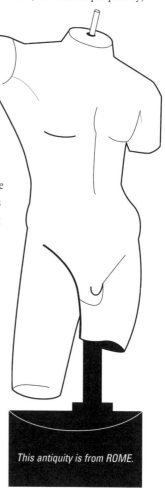

This antiquity is from ROME.

14

AT THE RACETRACK

This is another one of those nightclub things. On one hand, don't go. But on the other hand I know that some people really enjoy it. I'll just say one thing: it can be very (VERY!) hot outside. This is why I like to recommend an additional accessory along with the usual robe, rings, tunic and big stick. I'm talking about a goblet, which your attendants can fill with water, wine, whatever, because you don't want to rely on the refreshments stand at a time like this. My favorite goblets are jewel-encrusted: there's no way getting around how fancy they are and good they look. My opinion on where to find the sort of antiquity I mean? You guessed it: Italy!!! They always find something very special in the back room, and they'll bring it to you with a kiss of the ring!! But if you went in wearing a motorcycle helmet? Of course not. You see how it is—even the wrong hat will change the entire outlook on life. And we all want to succeed.

✣ **pope tip** *Don't go to the racetrack. But if you do, dress for success!!*

Jewel-encrusted is Best.

FANCY STATE DINNERS

OK, NOW THIS IS ONE place that I think we won't have any trouble with people saying, "Please, your Grace, I want to wear sandals!!" Fancy state dinners are a fact of life—diplomats, ambassadors (which are sort of the same thing), presidents, kings (not too many left of those!!) and other people are at these *very important dinners* and whether you're the Pope or not you want to look your best. So tell your attendants to get out a very fancy robe, and don't skimp on the rings!! If you have different tunics like we were saying before with the less fancy stitching, you might want to buy a fancy one for this, because it's a very special night and everybody will be looking at you and what you're wearing!!

When the soup comes, DON'T take off your hat. That's just silly and if that weren't enough, it might be messy, too. You don't have to worry too much about what to say—even though everybody's a big shot at these things, just general small talk will do. (Sooner or later people are going to come up with excommunication as a topic, and my advice is to say something like, "You know what? Let's just enjoy our lamb. The sauce is delicious, don't you think?") One thing that's a surefire pleaser is Italy and its rich history of antiquities (a great time to show off the scepter stick!!), what it's like in the Vatican, snow, etc.

✤ **pope tip** *With the tunic like we were saying before, BUY AHEAD. Nobody likes to hear, "Attendants, I need a super-fancy tunic by seven-thirty TONIGHT." If it's an emergency, of course, everybody will understand because everybody has to pitch in. But for regular? If a fancy state dinner has been on the calendar for a few weeks there is NO EXCUSE for not looking your BEST!!!!!!!!!!!*

THE BEACH

The beach is an interesting issue in terms of looking your best. On the one hand, it's the beach for Chrissakes!! Is there a more casual place in the whole earth??? But on the other hand, it's a place where you're going to be noticed. So that's why I'm going to be firm about this: NO SANDALS. "Your Holiness, Your Holiness, are you actually saying that people shouldn't wear sandals at the beach?" Look, I'm not saying NOBODY. I'm saying those who want to look their best. If you're just a lifeguard and you don't have any ambition in your life, then sure, wear sandals, I'm not going to pummel you with my staff. If you're one of those loose women in the bikini bathing suits you think looks so sexy but really looks awful? Sure. But if you're the Pope, you need to wear the robe, the tunic (short sleeves probably), fancy shoes and plenty of rings, and I see no reason why other people who want to LOOK THEIR BEST shouldn't follow suit. You might find me stubborn about this, but I only get stubborn about important things, and I think this is very important.

OK, LECTURE'S OVER!!!!!!!!!!!!!!

GOING TO THE MOVIES OR A PLAY

"EXCUSE ME, YOUR GRACE?" "Yes, Mario?" "I can't see the movie—your hat's in the way!!" If I had a few lire every time I heard that I would be redecorating the entire Vatican right now!! Does this mean, leave your hat at home? NO! Does this mean, take off your hat so the people behind you can see?? Not necessarily. Does this mean, arrange for a private showing of the movie? Now we're cooking!! Of course this isn't always possible—it depends on what you do. Pope? Yes. Archbishop? Probably. Priest? You're probably better talking to the archbishop to see what he can do! Nevertheless I'm going to go out on a limb and give private screenings my *primo recommendo!* But just because you're not actually in a movie theater doesn't mean you can sit around in sweats. Once again—I bet you can say it along with me—I'm talking about rings on your fingers, a big hat on your head and a robe and tunic on your main body. After all, a private screening is often full of important guests. This is another thing that's good to talk about at fancy state dinners—"OK, who here wants to see *Ocean's Eleven?*" That'll get the interest of royalty in a BIG WAY!!!

Do you see what I mean? Because it's the theme of the whole book. If you look good people will treat you good. That's the glory of my tips, Pope or no Pope: dress in your best hat, your best robe, plenty of good rings and yes, a good tunic too. And don't forget the scepter stick! For dramatic gestures, it makes a big hit. "AND NOW ... LET THE MOVIE BEGIN!"

✤ **pope tip** American Beauty *shouldn't have won all those Oscars.*

TRAVELING: BY AIRPLANE ESPECIALLY

THERE'S NO GETTING around it—in this modern world, airplanes are how people are getting around nowadays. People just aren't going to travel on a big oceanliner any more—it's a waste of time. And horseback? I don't think so!!!!

Just the other day an attendant said, "Your Grace, why don't we just pack up your fancy robe, pack up the shoes that curl at the toes, pack up your scepter staff and even pack up your tunic? When we arrive in Budapest you can change into your outfit at the hotel and you'll look fantastic for the Festival Mass!!" I was like, "Then you better pack me up too, because there is NO WAY I'm going to wear just regular 'hanging out' clothes on the plane! I want to look my best!!!" You should have seen all the blushing that this attendant did—I sure showed him!! If you looked up "bowing and scraping" in the dictionary there'd sure be a picture of this guy!!

Of course, not everybody takes a private jet. (Although I still think more people could if they just put their minds to it.) And if you're on regular airlines there's going to be some restrictions. But if you stepped aboard an airplane wearing a fancy robe with really shiny stitching, a tunic underneath, a big hat and a stick with a nice curve on the top, do you honestly think that the stewardess lady is going to give you grief??? Fat chance, *mio fratello!* More like an upgrade. And don't forget the rings. Just take them off when they ask and put them through the X-ray, and then put them back on, all over your hands. You look great!!!

CHRISTMASTIME

OK, WE'RE ALMOST AT the end of the book and I hope you've learned a few things. I thought it was appropriate to save the best for last—Christmas! (After all, it's almost at the end of the year.) Christmas of course is a very moving time and it's a special time too. Whether you're first in line for Midnight Mass or if you just stay home this year and spend some "primo time" with your family, Christmas is a time for togetherness, love, eating together with family and/or friends, opening presents, a tree, and ... that's right!! Looking your best! Of all the days in the year to skimp on robes, this isn't it. In fact, I like to save a special robe just for Christmas I call "the fancy Christmas robe."

"Your Worship, is there any particular robe you're thinking off?" My red robe, of course. For some reason over history, red and green have become the semi-official colors of Christmas. Green, you have all over the place—wreaths, etc. But red ... well, let's just say that when the red robe goes on, I honestly don't think I could look any better. And I'm sure it's the same with you. Add a few rings with red shiny stones, polish up that ruby goblet, even get a tunic with some red stitching if the tunic shows through. You also might invest in a big staff (or scepter) with red decorations that shine like the big star of Christmas itself. What's the perfect thing to top off a Christmas outfit like this? A big hat, of course.

Merry Christmas to everyone, and don't forget the shoes.

✣ **pope tip** *Oftentimes people decorate with poinsettias which are a sort of "Christmas plant." Have an attendant hold up your robe next to a poinsettia. Does it clash? Are the reds slightly off? Then I'm afraid you've got the wrong robe.*

Does it CLASH??

25

GLOSSARY

This is a list of different words from the book, along with their meanings, in the order of me thinking of them.

THE POPE: Me! Head of the Vatican. (Nicknames: Your Holiness, Your Grace.)

THE VATICAN: It's sort of Italy, it's sort of not. It's hard to explain. It's basically a big, big set of buildings where I live. Also it's my work place. For more details see: THE POPE.

EDICT: Very important pieces of paper where I write stuff down.

FANCY SHOES: A must for the feet. Part of the basic outfit.

SANDALS: The opposite of Fancy Shoes. Sort of strappy, lazy things that people just throw on their feet for anytime. Not part of snappy dressing at all!!!

ANTIQUITY: An old thing, usually from Italy.

ITALY: The country where I live, if you don't count the Vatican. (See: VATICAN.)

CURLED-UP TOES: A very important part of the shoe. (See: SHOES.) The ends of the shoes sort of curl up, like a curly wave. The illustrations would really explain it better!!!

ILLUSTRATIONS: Drawings for this book. Special thanks to Pinkie!!!!

ATTENDANTS: People to help you. Usually hired by Vatican guys or I think some kind of agency. Ask for details!!!!

STICK: Other word for "Scepter Staff." It's the basic thing you hold as part of the outfit. It's not just a regular stick!!! Look at the illustrations.

BOWL OF INCENSE: Optional.

POPE TIP: Helpful things for you. See: THE POPE.

SNAPPY DRESSING: One of the most important things in the book! Basically, it's trying to look your best—not in a show-offy way, but just regular, snappy dressing. Parts of snappy dressing include the hat, the stick, a robe, tunics and fancy shoes. (See also: RINGS.)

TUNIC: A shirt, usually with stitching. It goes under robes.

ROBES: What you wear on the main body.

POPE HAT: A tall hat worn by Popes (See: THE POPE) and also a part of snappy dressing (See: LOOKING YOUR BEST).

LOOKING YOUR BEST: Super-important!! Includes hat, fancy shoes, rings, a tunic, robes and of course the scepter stick!!!

EXCOMMUNICATION: A tricky topic, not really put in this book. (See: THE POPE for more info.)

CHRISTMAS: Hooray for Christmas! A very special time.

FREQUENTLY ASKED QUESTIONS

Q: *Is it really all that important to dress your very best?*
A: Um, HELLO?!?! Yes! Next question please!!!!

Q: *I'm a woman. Sometimes I have to dress differently.*
A: SO WHAT?? Be yourself!!!

Q: *Does the hat come in adjustable sizes?*
A: Don't skimp on the hat. Get a hat—if it fits, great, if it doesn't fit, get another hat.

Q: *Some of these outfits seem a little dressy.*
A: I know.

Q: *Once and for all, what is the position of the Catholic Church on Israel?*
A: Let's stick to the topic please!!!!!!

Q: *I don't really have a question. I just wanted to thank you.*
A: You're welcome!!! And thank you too!!!